A MINI-POSTER BOOK

COMPILATION
CYNTHIA HART

PHOTOGRAPHS
GEOFFREY BIDDLE/ARCHIVE

TEXT
JOE RUDDICK
AND
ANI SCHEMPF

Skateboarding involves a high degree of physical risk. This book is not in any way intended to be an instructional book on skateboarding. Proper instruction, training, and safety equipment should be obtained before anyone participates in this sport.

SCHOLASTIC INC.
New York Toronto London Auckland Sydney

GLOSSARY

Air: A trick done while suspended in the air.

Bail: To intentionally abandon a trick when the skater has lost control.

Half-pipe: A style of ramp with vertical sides at both ends.

Jam: A free-form group skating session.

Lip: The top edge of a ramp.

Ollie: A trick where the skater pulls air from the street or a ramp, with both feet on the board.

Plant: (also Invert) Balancing with one hand on the ground or lip of a ramp.

Pulling air: Defying gravity. Taking off from a ramp for maximum climb.

Ramp: A large, curved wooden structure, especially designed for skaters to launch themselves into moments of gravity-defying free flight.

Shred: To perform with great intensity and skill.

Skate: n.: a skateboard (also Board, Stick).
v.: to ride a skateboard.

Slam: To crash or fall.

Stoked: Excited, happy, satisfied.

Transition: The curved part(s) of a ramp.

With special thanks to Harumi

Scholastic Books are available at special discounts for quantity purchases for use as premiums, promotional items, retail sales through specialty market outlets, etc. For details contact: Special Sales Manager, Scholastic Inc., 730 Broadway, New York, NY 10003.

Book Design: Hollie A. Rubin

ISBN 0-590-41150-0

Compilation copyright © 1988 by Cynthia Hart. Cover photo © Geoffrey Biddle. All rights reserved. Published by Scholastic Inc.

12 11 10 9 8 7 6 5 4 3 2 1   8 9/8 0 1 2 3/9

Printed in the U.S.A.

First Scholastic printing, January 1988

Your skateboard can be bought ready-made or assembled from parts. Every item can be an important choice: the deck (with a wild paint job), trucks (axle assemblies), wheels, bearings, and grip tape (like sandpaper stuck to the board—so you don't slide off!). Plastic accessories—copers, lappers, noseguard, tail, and rails—are attached to protect the hardware and the deck. Stickers can make a very personal statement. Here, Tony Phongsy puts his skate to good use.

0-590-41150-0 Published by Scholastic Inc., 730 Broadway, New York, NY 10003.
© Geoffrey Biddle

Skateboarding first became popular in California during the sixties. It was invented by some surfers who tried to capture on land the feeling of riding an ocean wave. Now, there are more than 30 million skaters across the country and around the world. Today, skateboarding has a style all its own, but many surfing moves and expressions are still used by skaters.

0-590-41150-0 Published by Scholastic Inc., 730 Broadway, New York, NY 10003.
© Geoffrey Biddle

Street and freestyle skaters concentrate on fancy moves close to the ground. There are hundreds of tricks using curbs, sidewalks, benches, even trees. Here, Christian Hosoi does a cool street plant. Countless hours of practice have earned him the athletic skills of a gymnast, the timing and flexibility of an acrobat, and the grace of a ballet dancer.

0-590-41150-0 Published by Scholastic Inc., 730 Broadway, New York, NY 10003.
© Geoffrey Biddle

Ramp-building originated in the seventies. For the first time, aerial skaters controlled their own skating environment. With a little money and a lot of time, perseverance, and resourcefulness, many skaters have built personal ramps or participated in community ramp projects.

The essence of ramp-skating—performing incredible tricks (somersaults, twists, and plants) while suspended in midair. Arms spread out like the wings of a bird, colorful Jeff Jones goes for maximum hang time with this ollie air. With his feet on the board the whole way, he'll spin 180 degrees in the air and land skating *fast* on the down ramp.

0-590-41150-0 Published by Scholastic Inc., 730 Broadway, New York, NY 10003.
All rights reserved. Printed in the U.S.A.
© Geoffrey Biddle

Build up speed on the straightaway, pumping with your legs. Rush up the transition. Just before the rear wheels hit the lip of the ramp, grab your board and hold tight while you pull maximum air. As you fly free, make a lightning-fast 180-degree spin. Let go of your board as you land already zooming to your next trick at the other end of the half-pipe. Imagine all this happening in five seconds, and you have the idea of Steve Caballero's backside air.

New York City "sky scraper!" Street skater Ian Frahm
grabs some spectacular air in Washington Square Park.

0-590-41150-0 Published by Scholastic Inc., 730 Broadway, New York, NY 10003.
© Geoffrey Biddle

A powerful trio of pro skaters—skateboard manufacturer Powell & Peralta's Lance Mountain, Steve Caballero, and Tony Hawk. With product endorsements, prize money, manufacturer's sponsorships, appearances in films and commercials—some of the best skating pros can earn over $100,000 a year!

0-590-41150-0 Published by Scholastic Inc., 730 Broadway, New York, NY 10003.

© Geoffrey Biddle

Skaters in the year 2000, watch out! Lance and Yvette Mountain's son, Lance Mountain, Jr., has a definite advantage in having a top skating pro for his dad. At age 1½, he's already getting the special feel and balance necessary for successful skating.

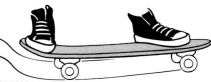

0-590-41150-0 Published by Scholastic Inc., 730 Broadway, New York, NY 10003.
© Geoffrey Biddle

A fantastic frontside invert. The longer Lenny Byrd can hold this stall, the better the trick. Next, he will push off and flip over, landing back on the ramp skating at high speed.

0-590-41150-0 Published by Scholastic Inc., 730 Broadway, New York, NY 10003.

© Geoffrey Biddle

Aerial tricks like rocket airs, frontsides, backsides, judos, and laybacks (to name just a few) require a lot of serious practice. Long after sunset, Jason Espeseth goes for ramp skating perfection at the Houston Skate Park.

0-590-41150-0 Published by Scholastic Inc., 730 Broadway, New York, NY 10003.

ni Schempf, Helen Wetherill, Jonny Zahourek, and Pollyn Caballero have a jam, a free-form skating session. No winners, no losers. Just the time and the place and the freedom to *shred* with other dedicated skaters. Above all, skateboarding means having a great time.

0-590-41150-0 Published by Scholastic Inc., 730 Broadway, New York, NY 10003.
© Geoffrey Biddle